Dancing with Tex

The Remarkable Friendship
To Save The Whooping Cranes

Written By: Lynn Sanders

Illustrated By: Sergio Drumond

Illustrations by Sergio Drumond.

Published by Difference Makers Media.
Bringing Your Stories to Life.

For information, contact Lynn Sanders at lynn@DifferenceMakersMedia.com.

www.DifferenceMakersMedia.com
www.DancingWithTex.com

ISBN-10: 0-9975921-1-7
ISBN-13: 978-0-9975921-1-5

First Edition

Publisher's Cataloging-In-Publication Data
(Prepared by The Donohue Group, Inc.)

Names: Sanders, Lynn Bogen. | Drumond, Sergio, illustrator.

Title: Dancing with Tex : the remarkable friendship to save the whooping cranes / written by: Lynn Sanders ; illustrated by: Sergio Drumond.

Description: First edition. | [Winnetka, Illinois] : Difference Makers Media, [2016] | Includes questions and answers section, vocabulary list, and discussion guide. | Interest age level: 006-010. | Summary: "Dancing With Tex tells the true story of friendship between a man and bird that led to helping save the Whooping Cranes from extinction."--Provided by publisher.

Identifiers: ISBN 978-0-9975921-1-5 (paperback) | ISBN 0-9975921-1-7 (paperback) | ISBN 978-0-9975921-2-2 (hardcover) | ISBN 0-9975921-2-5 (hardcover)

Subjects: LCSH: Whooping crane--Conservation--Juvenile literature. | Archibald, George--Juvenile literature. | Endangered species--Juvenile literature. | Courtship in animals--Juvenile literature. | Human-animal relationships--Juvenile literature. | Dance--Juvenile literature. | CYAC: Whooping crane. | Archibald, George. | Endangered species. | Animals--Courtship. | Human-animal relationships. | Dance.

Classification: LCC QL676.2 .S26 2016 (print) | LCC QL676.2 (ebook) | DDC 598.3/2 [E]--dc23

Introduction

""We should care for the land and the life it supports, so the land will always sustain life… Not everyone can dance with Whooping Cranes, but we all can do a dance to promote life on earth." George Archibald, Co-Founder of The International Crane Foundation, Baraboo, Wisconsin.

This is the true story of two special friends: a man named George who loved birds and a bird named Tex who loved people.

No one could have guessed the two would someday become dance partners. George never took a single dancing lesson.

No one could have guessed the two would someday be world-famous. They lived in the small town of Baraboo, Wisconsin.

And no one could have guessed their dancing would make a difference in saving the Whooping Cranes from extinction. How much could one bird and one man do?

But George and Tex believed in each other, helped each other and never gave up. Their friendship made a difference.

You can make a difference too.

Decide what it is you want to do. Choose a friend who believes in you to support your dreams. Then never give up and see what happens.

JULY 9, 1972

Under a blazing sun at the San Antonio Zoo,

a special egg slowly opens. Fred, the zookeeper,

watches carefully.

Tiny holes.

Tiny cracks.

Tiny sounds.

"**Cheep! Cheep!**"

She is one of the rarest birds,

a **Whooping Crane**.

"Welcome to Texas, little Tex!" said Fred.

"You'll be safe at my place."

Reaching down, Fred gently lifted Tex

into a cardboard box and hurried home.

Fred kept Tex warm, gave her water and fed her tasty food. Tex didn't see another bird for 16 days. Since **newborn** animals believe whoever watches over them is family, **Tex believed she belonged with people, not birds.**

A visiting scientist told Fred, "Tex must live with her own kind. Otherwise, she will never lay an egg." Fred knew every egg mattered. Only a small number of Whooping Cranes lived on earth.

Cheep!

If Tex hatched a chick, more Whooping Cranes could be born. They could save the **species** from dying off forever.

"Sorry, Tex," said Fred, "You have to go."

"**Cheep**!" said Tex.

Off Tex went to live in a big **wildlife research center** in Maryland. Here, she could wander in grassy fields and make new bird friends. But did she? *NO WAY!* Years passed and Tex became very lonely. The problem was...

Cheep!
Cheep!

As a newborn chick, Tex never saw another Whooping Crane taking care of her. Instead, Tex only saw Fred. So Tex's brain was **imprinted** by a person. She thought people were her family...especially anyone who looked like Fred.

One day, a student named George Archibald came to the center for a visit. He had raised birds on his family's farm in Canada since he was small. George loved birds as much as Tex loved people, and he wanted to save all the cranes.

George knew Whooping Cranes would disappear if more chicks weren't born. Tex was getting older. It would be harder for her to lay an egg.

"Tex, what if I could help you?" George asked.

"Ker-loo!" Tex answered.

Back at school, George and his friend Ron made a plan.
They decided to build a place to keep all cranes safe.
"Maybe my parents could help us," Ron said.

Sure enough, Ron's parents did help. They let George and Ron use their empty horse farm in Baraboo, Wisconsin. All cranes would now have a safe home. **No one had ever done that before!** It was named *The International Crane Foundation.* With many helping hands, George, Ron and their friends built bird sheds on the land.

They asked scientists to send cranes and wrote letters. Fourteen different **species** of cranes arrived from around the world. Only the rarest type of crane was missing: **The Whooping Crane.** George was hoping Tex could join the other cranes. Would it be possible to move Tex?

APRIL 15, 1976

YES! Tex arrived at her new home.

Crowds gathered.

Cameras flashed.

Reporters took notes.

For the first time in **100** years,

a **Whooping Crane**

lived in *Wisconsin.*

Now it was time for George to help **TEX** lay an egg. **It could save her SPECIES!**

George knew all cranes dance together before laying an egg, but they only dance with partners they like.

So George arranged to have **TONY**, another **Whooping Crane**, join Tex in a nearby shed.

Since **TEX** was **imprinted** on people, would she dance with **TONY?**

NO WAY!

George knew how cranes danced from studying them at school. This gave him an idea…

"Would Tex

DANCE with **ME**?"

George wondered.

"Let's find out," said Ron.

To help Tex like him as a new dance partner, George decided to move into her shed. Ron helped George carry his bed, desk, and chair inside.

"Good luck!" said Ron.

George turned to Tex. "Can we be friends?"

"**KER-LOO!**" Tex nodded her head.

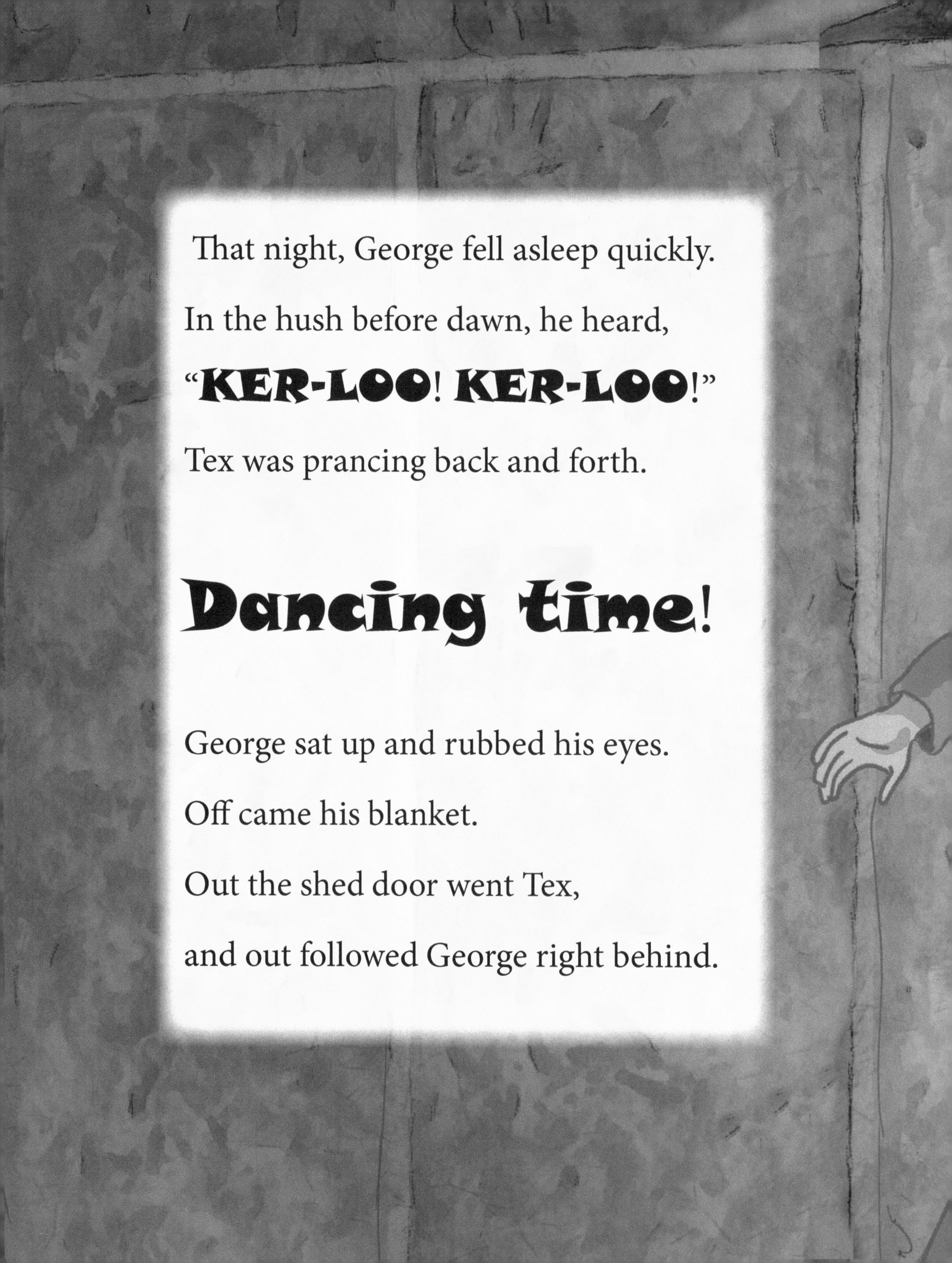

That night, George fell asleep quickly.

In the hush before dawn, he heard,

"KER-LOO! KER-LOO!"

Tex was prancing back and forth.

Dancing time!

George sat up and rubbed his eyes.

Off came his blanket.

Out the shed door went Tex,

and out followed George right behind.

"**KER-LOO**!" Tex sang.
She jumped, flapped her wings and bowed.
"**TEX**!" declared George.
He jumped, flapped his arms and bowed.

They **danced and danced and danced**.
Finally, Tex rested.
"Whew!" George said.
His knees were sore. His back ached.

Ker-loo!

Soon, Tex wanted to **dance again!**

After they danced, George asked two scientists to hide behind the shed. When George gave them a sign, they moved close to Tex. One held Tex still, while the other gave her a special shot. Tex didn't like it, but it had to be done. This **injection** could help her lay an egg.

George and Tex **danced** and **danced** a lot that spring, but Tex didn't lay an egg.

"Let's try again next year," George said.

"**KER-LOO!**" answered Tex.

SPRING 1977

George and Tex **danced** and **danced**.

Again, scientists gave Tex special shots.

This time it worked. Tex laid an egg! Woo-Hoo!

But the good news quickly turned into bad news.

George checked Tex's egg under a bright light.

Something was wrong.

There was no chick inside.

"Oh well," George sighed. "Let's try again next year."

SPRING 1978 & 1979

Before long, it was spring again. George and Tex **danced** and **danced**. Tex laid another egg, but the unborn chick died before hatching.

The next spring, Tex's eggshell was too soft.

"SO sorry Tex," George said. "We must keep trying."

SPRING 1980 & 1981

Unfortunately for Tex, George needed to help save the cranes in other places. He arranged to have two scientists, first Yoshi and then Mike, dance with Tex. Tex only danced with Mike, but it didn't matter. She still didn't lay an egg!

SPRING 1982

Six years had passed. George was NOT giving up!

Once again, he moved into Tex's shed.

"**KER-LOO-OO-OOO!**" Tex sang,

flapping her

giant wings.

"Let's

DANCE,

Tex!"

called

George,

waving his

arms.

How they **DANCED**

      and DANCED

           and DANCED until...

TEX DID IT! She laid a **fertile** egg!

It was small, wrinkled, and had a strange shape.

The egg needed to be cared for in an **incubator.**

Ron and George didn't know if the chick inside

would survive.

JUNE 1, 1982

One summer day in Baraboo, Wisconsin,

A very special egg starts to open.

George and Ron noticed something.

Tiny holes.

Tiny cracks.

Tiny sounds.

"Cheep! Cheep!"

A new Whooping Crane chick pushed out of his shell.

George smiled.

"Hello **Gee Whiz**! Welcome to the world!

We've been waiting a *LONG TIME* for you!"

Gee Whiz eventually became a father to 15 chicks and 44 grand chicks. Those chicks helped keep the Whooping Cranes alive today. Thanks to George and Tex, the Whooping Cranes still live on the earth! It happened because George and Tex never gave up. They believed in each other, and that made the difference.

Isn't that what friends are for?

Author's Note

I met George during a video project for The International Crane Foundation and fell in love with this magical place. As I heard the cranes calling, it felt like I stepped back in time. When George told me about Tex, I knew it would make a perfect children's story. It's inspiring to learn how you can make your dreams come true by having belief, faith, and never giving up.

George and Ron's non-profit organization, The International Crane Foundation (ICF) in Baraboo, Wisconsin, remains the only place in the world that cares for all fifteen species of cranes. It has become what George imagined -- a leader in saving the world's cranes.

Known by scientists as "The World's Ambassador for the Cranes," Dr. George Archibald has saved several crane species from extinction. He received many awards and was inducted in Wisconsin's Conservation Hall of Fame.

The International Crane Foundation covers 225 acres, and each year, over 25,000 guests visit the world headquarters. Visitors enjoy live crane exhibits, tours, an education center, visitor's center, a research library and over four miles of nature trails. Everyone is welcome!

Today, just like his cranes, George continues flying across the globe to speak out. Many cranes -- including the Whooping Cranes -- are still endangered. George teaches people how to save cranes and protect their land and water. Since cranes travel across many countries, George's work brings people from different nations together. By saving cranes, George hopes to build peace and understanding among all people.

In Japanese legends, the crane lives one thousand years. That's why the crane is a symbol for long life, good luck and happiness. Crane pictures can be found on screens, prints, airlines, ceramics, rugs, and notecards. The Whooping Cranes, like other crane species, still face the danger of extinction. Only by working together can we keep cranes alive. You can help too. Learn how to adopt a crane at www.savingcranes.org.

Lynn Sanders

LYNN SANDERS

About the Author

Lynn Sanders, Founder & President of Difference Makers Media is a story marketing expert, whose passion is creating, telling and sharing inspiring stories that make a positive impact. Her coaching, writing, marketing and media helps entrepreneurs and non-profit leaders expand their exposure, build their impact, and attract revenue. Lynn is the author of the children's non-fiction book, "Social Justice: How You Can Make A Difference," published by Capstone Press. To learn more about attracting results from your stories, visit DifferenceMakersMedia.com.

About the Illustrator

Sergio Drumond is a painter, illustrator, animator and digital graphic artist who has worked for clients around the world. His worldwide experiences includes studies at: Escola de Belas Artes in Bahia, Illustration and Commercial Arts at SENAC, painting at Goethe Institut, under German painter Adam Firnekaes, and engraving with engraver and Art Museum curator, Emanuel Araujo. Sergio's portfolio includes illustrating for advertisements, books, posters, magazines, newspapers and television.

SERGIO DRUMOND

Acknowledgements

Many people helped bring this story to life. I'm grateful to each of you.

First, a huge thanks to Dr. George Archibald, co-founder of the International Crane Foundation, for sharing his story with me many years ago and answering my questions. George, your belief, faith and perseverance not only continues to protect the cranes, but you inspired me to publish this story.

Thanks to my parents, Gil and Rosalyn Bogen, who believed in its value and encouraged me to keep going. I'm also indebted to my late friend, dear Bobette Zacharias, whose support helped make this book a reality. Of course, I can't leave out my husband, Joel and sons Jordan and Andrew who motivated me to never give up.

Several years ago, this story was developed into a children's musical, "A Whooper's Tale: The Incredible Story of Tex." To my musical collaborators: Jenny Stafford and Russ Coutinho -- "Ker-loo!" You brought such fun and joy in creating this story into a children's musical.

For the many contributors on my Indiegogo crowdfunding site: I couldn't have done it without you.

A heartfelt note of gratitude to Rick Fox, former board member at ICF, for his ongoing faith in this work. Thanks to: Polly Vinograd, Elaine Nieberding, Sandy Mosetick, Gregory Hubert, Steve & Drorit Bogen, Mark & Kathleen Bogen, Judy Heller Moeller, Glen Strauss, Linda Kroll, Cari Alexander, Charlene Novak, Bonnie Gibson, Steve Taubman, Donna Schwarzbach and David Gordon, Louis & Sheri Schwarzbach, Jan Stringer & Alan Hickman, Sandy Ben-Zev, Beth Ellis, Leslie & Jeff Newcorn, Dana McLaughlin, Karen Taylor-Good, Rayne Dowell, Manolis Sfinarolakis, Roland Takaoka, Hilton Hotel in Baraboo, The San Antonio Zoo and KSTP News for their video footage. I also appreciated the editorial feedback and critiques from authors Marlene Brill, Esther Hershenhorn, Susan Bearman and Janie Baskin.

I'm grateful for the input from thoughtful colleagues who took their time to do research, digging up photos and uncovering information. Thank you, Josef San Miguel, Elizabeth Castillo and Dawn Koehler at the San Antonio Zoo; John French and Mark Wimer at Patuxent Wildlife Research Center and Mary Guthrie at Cornell University.

Of course, this story would never have been possible if it weren't for the thoughtfulness of videographer Rick Erwin, who hired me to be the writer/co-producer on his Amoco project about The International Crane Foundation.

An angel in disguise came to me in the form of Ann Knipp, of Chicago Kids Media. Thank you, Ann for your editorial consulting and formatting of this book. I appreciate you so much.

Last but definitely not least, I want to thank my amazing illustrator, Sergio Drumond. You captured the story beautifully, and have been a delight to collaborate with. I'm so glad I found you.

May this story live on in the hearts of children. It demonstrates the need to protect our environment and never give up on your dreams. Just as George and Tex made a positive difference in the world, I encourage readers to follow their dreams, so we can help make this earth a better place.

Remember: Never give up! If I did it, so can you.

Questions & Answers

#1: Where was George born?

George was born in New Glasgow, a scenic town built along the banks of the East River, on the northern shore of Nova Scotia, Canada.

#2: What did George's family do?

George's parents, Donald and Lettie Archibald were teachers, who encouraged their six children to follow their own interests. When the children were born, Lettie retired from teaching to care for Ann, George, Donald, Heather, Sandy and Peter.

#3: What were some of George's favorite childhood memories?

George cared for his own birds in sheds, and loved watching gulls fly down to grab food from his hands. He also enjoyed Schubenacadie Wildlife Nature Preserve, where wild and tame animals live together.

#4: How far do cranes fly?

The crane family flies over five of the seven continents, except South America and Antarctica.

#5: Why did George decide to study at Cornell University to become a bird scientist?

George read about Cornell University's Bird Laboratory in National Geographic. The story made him realize he wanted to become a bird scientist (an ornithologist). George chose Cornell because it is one of the best schools in the world for ornithology.

#6: What happened during George's first visit to Cornell?

Since he didn't have much money to visit, George walked and hitchhiked from Montreal, Canada to Cornell University in Ithaca, New York. The distance was about 300 miles! George met Professor Dilger who encouraged him to apply, and the rest is history!

#7: What was the name of the wildlife center where Tex lived?

Patuxent Wildlife Research Center in Laurel, Maryland. Opening in 1936, Patuxent is America's first and only wildlife refuge, dedicated to studying wildlife and their environment.

#8: How tall are Whooping Cranes and how did they get their name?

Whooping Cranes are 5 feet tall, the tallest flying birds in North America. They got their name because their call sounds like a "whoop!"

#9: How did George communicate with Tex?

Since Tex identified with people, George spoke to Tex in English. He did not try to sound like a crane.

#10: Why did Fred Stark, the San Antonio zoo director, bring Tex to his home?

Fred wanted to protect Tex because he knew she was rare. Before Tex was born, her mother, Rosie, had laid two eggs. Tex's father, Crip, accidentally stepped on the first baby chick. Fred was determined to keep Tex safe from an accident.

#11: How many eggs do Whooping Cranes usually produce at one time?

Most Whooping cranes lay two eggs. When Tex finally began laying eggs, she laid one egg at a time.

#12: How did Gee Whiz get his name?

Gee Whiz was named after Dr. George Gee, who helped provide the injections to help Tex lay an egg. The "whiz" was added because everyone was surprised when Tex finally hatched a chick.

#13: Why do cranes dance?

Cranes dance to show happiness, protect their home, get rid of nervous feelings, and to attract a partner. Each type of crane dances in his or her own way. Dancing builds a friendly relationship between pairs of birds. When cranes choose a partner, they usually keep the same one for life.

#14: Why is it important to save the cranes and all endangered animals?

We believe all life is connected – people, animals and plants. That's why we need to care for each other. We each affect each other. When we save cranes, who have lived on earth since prehistoric times, we're also protecting our land and water. Since cranes fly across different countries, in order to save cranes, people from different backgrounds must cooperate. Thanks to the cranes, we can learn to build bridges of peace across the world.

#15: Why do species become extinct, and how many are endangered?

The biggest reason behind the loss of animals and plants is people! Over the last 500 years, people have caused harm through pollution, hunting and destroying natural habitats.
As of 2016, our world has 16,306 endangered species (plants and animals) who face extinction.
In the United States alone, there are 750 plants and 574 animals who are endangered.
(See: www.EndangeredEarth.com) We all must speak up to protect our world. Extinct species will never return!

#16: What can you do to care for endangered animals?

There are many things you can do to care for endangered animals:
- Recycle as much as possible to reduce pollution and help protect habitats.
- Avoid using pesticide on your lawn which adds harmful chemicals in the air.
- Volunteer at parks, nature centers and wilderness areas.
- Support zoos and aquariums.
- Write letters or call government leaders to speak up about saving our land and animals..
- Support endangered species online who need it most.
- Visit: www.biologicaldiversity.org to learn more.

The World of Cranes

Black Crowned Crane

Black-Necked Crane

Blue Crane

Brolga Crane

Demoiselle Crane

Red-Crowned Crane

Sandhill Crane

Sarus Crane

Siberian Crane

Wattled Crane

Eurasian Crane

Grey Crowned Crane

Hooded Crane

White-Naped Crane

Whooping Crane

Helpful Vocabulary Words

1. **Candling** - Looking inside the shell of an egg to check if it's fertile by holding it up to a bright light or candle.
2. **Embryo** - An unborn human or animal in its early stages before birth.
3. **Endangered** - When an animal is at serious risk of becoming extinct.
4. **Extinct** - When a type of animal dies off and disappears forever.
5. **Fertile** - An egg that carries life inside it.
6. **Habitat** - The place where an animal lives.
7. **Imprinting** - (Scientific meaning) When an animal recognizes another person, animal or object as their parent or family.
8. **Incubator** - A machine with a chamber that provides controlled temperature and humidity conditions. An incubator can be used to hatch eggs, to protect sick babies, or to care for those who are born too early.
9. **Injection** - Forcing a substance into someone or something using a special needle.
10. **Newborn** - A recently born baby.
11. **Ornithologist** - A scientist who specializes in studying birds.
12. **Species** - A group of animals or plants who are similar.

Discussion Guide

We each make a difference in the world.

It's up to us to choose our beliefs, our attitude, and what we want to do with our lives. From my own experience, I urge you -- never give up on your dreams. The world needs more dreamers who want to create a better world. We need people like you!

After reading Dancing With Tex, you may want to have a conversation around these questions.

1. Can people be imprinted in a positive or negative way by those around them?

2. Why was Ron's friendship so special for George? Why do we need friends?

3. Why do you think George moved into Tex's shed? What did that show Tex?

4. Why did George keep trying to help Tex lay a fertile egg?

5. Do you remember a time when you didn't give up? How did you feel?

6. What happens when a species becomes extinct?

7. Why must we do what we can to save our endangered species?

8. Why do we need to protect the environment? What can you do?

9. Many people go through failures before their dreams become successful. What can we learn from our failures? Why is it important to never give up?

10. What would you like to do to make this a better world?

Get Inspired

1. Every success begins with believing in yourself. What do you choose to believe in?

_____
_____
_____

2. Your brain listens to everything you say. Pretend you're coaching yourself to handle any problem. What positive messages can you tell yourself?

_____
_____
_____

3. Write how you feel when you have faith in yourself.

_____
_____
_____

4. To reach your dreams, it's important to never give up. Can you name some people in history who never gave up?

_____
_____
_____

5. What can you do now that can help others?

_____
_____
_____

6. Imagine you have a magic wand to create the perfect future. What would you be doing?

_____
_____
_____

What People are Saying

"We're glad to see a book that helps connect young people with endangered birds. Every one of those connections is an opportunity to spark a new conversation, save another species and leave behind a world that's still full of wonder and the wild."

Kieran Suckling, Executive Director, Center for Biological Diversity.

"A unique story wrapped up in a wonderfully illustrated book with a special message for the conservation of cranes."

Roger Lederer, Founder of Ornithology.com.

"I loved this fascinating true story about the transformational power behind a unique friendship. Inspiring for children too!"

Sonia Choquette, Globally Celebrated and Dynamic Spiritual Teacher, Consultant, Storyteller, and Transformational Visionary Guide.

"George Archibald has inspired me and many others through his accomplishments and dedication. This delightful, charmingly illustrated story of his experiences with Tex shows young readers the value of hard work, persistence and friendship."

Jane Chandler, Patuxent Crane Flock Manager, 1990-2014.

George Archibald & Tex. reprinted with permission from the International Crane Foundation.

CPSIA information can be obtained
at www.ICGtesting.com
Printed in the USA
LVHW05s0955020618
579333LV00007B/11/P